MACHINE EMBROIDE[RY]
Special Occasions

Joan Hinds

©2007 by Joan Hinds
Published by

krause publications
An Imprint of F+W Publications

**700 East State Street • Iola, WI 54990-0001
715-445-2214 • 888-457-2873
www.krausebooks.com**

Our toll-free number to place an order or obtain a free catalog is (800) 258-0929.

The following trademarked terms and companies appear in this publication: Aurifil™, Beacon Flip-flop Glue, Camelot Cottons, CheepTrims.com, Fray Block®, Insul-Bright®, Madeira USA, Mary's Productions, RNK Distributing, Robert Kaufman Fabrics, Robison-Anton®, Sulky of America®, Superior Threads, Timeless Treasures Fabrics, Inc., Velcro®

Library of Congress Catalog Number: 2006935581

ISBN: 978-0-89689-484-6

Designed by
Heidi Bittner-Zastrow

Edited by Erica Swanson

Printed in China

Dedication

To my mother, Nina Sudor,
party planner extraordinaire, for her continuing inspiration.

Acknowledgments

I have enjoyed spreading my wings in this book with machine embroidery. I want to thank the companies listed in the Resources section, pg. 126, for their generous support and contributions of fabric and embroidery products. I also want to thank the following individuals for their help and support:

My illustrator, Kathy Marsaa, for her fabulous interpretations of my embroidery ideas.

Jay Fishman, from Wicked Stitch of the East, Inc., for his beautiful digitized designs, as well as his unending patience.

Marilee Sagat, for her assistance with design and construction techniques, as well as her friendship.

The staff at Krause Publications, including my editor Erica Swanson, Susan Sliwicki, Candy Wiza, and photographers Bob Best and Kris Kandler for making this book possible.

Lynn Mann Hallmark, for her photo styling expertise.

Lastly, to my husband Fletcher and daughter Rebecca, who answered the calls for design or color decisions at all hours of the night.

Contents

Introduction

Hosting a party can be wonderfully creative, especially if you add festive embroidery to your table linens and decorations. Your event can be a simple dinner party for four, a family birthday party or a beach party bash — every get-together can become more personalized when you create your own decorations!

The idea for this book came one day as I pulled out the generic plastic tablecloth and paper products I had used for each family member's birthday party. I realized how unattractive the tablecloth was, and how wasteful it was to use all the paper items. That's when I decided to create beautiful and reusable decorations for birthdays and other occasions.

I have designed eight party themes with decorations and table linens for your events. You can choose to use all of the ideas presented in one of the themes, or perhaps just one or two of them. You can even combine projects from several themes to create your own special party décor. The machine embroidery designs included for each theme are used to decorate the projects. Whether you are an embroidery machine expert or a beginner, these designs can be mixed and matched to suit your needs. Some of the projects have been created from scratch, while others are purchased items that have simply been decorated with my machine embroidery designs. This will give you flexibility in how much sewing you want to do for your own event. I found most of the materials for the various projects in craft or party stores, so you should have no trouble finding the perfect supplies.

Many projects can be created for each theme if you combine my ideas with your own. Decorating and designing your own decorations will make get-togethers even more special. Your guests will be talking about your parties for years!

Getting Started
Equipment, Fabric and Supplies

To make these fantastic projects, you will need to have an embroidery sewing machine. The designs are included in the CD at the back of the book for you to convert for your machine. The stitching order with colors is also included in .pdf form for you to use as a guide.

Gather the basic essential equipment: a cutting mat and rotary cutter, shears, sewing and embroidery needles, iron, rulers, temporary spray adhesive and seam sealant. For the embroidery, you will need stabilizers of all kinds, such as cut-away, adhesive, tear-away and wash-away, bobbin thread and bobbins, and hoops in the 4" and 5" x 7" sizes. Machine embroidery thread is available in both polyester and rayon. Be sure to check for the washability of your thread if you plan to wash any of the projects. A double-curved pointed scissors is helpful for cutting the threads in the hoop. Nylon fabric, such as organza, can be used for stand-alone appliqués. A hot knife or hot textile tool melts the fabric from the edges of the embroidery.

I have used mostly quilting cotton prints and solids in my projects due to the fabulous coordinating prints that fit my party themes. I have also used other fabrics, such as satin and linen, with good results. Machine embroidery works well on many types of fabrics.

For the best results (and to reduce frustration), I highly recommend testing each design before you begin a project. Use the fabrics, threads and stabilizers that you will be using for your actual project to see how the design will look. Then, adjust colors, needles and stabilizers before completing the final version.

Handmade or Ready-made?

Table linens can be completely handmade and decorated with machine embroidery, or they can be purchased as finished items and then machine embroidered — it's up to you! If you find the perfect fabric for your party, go ahead and make all of your linens. If you find the ideal plain tablecloth or napkins (often called blanks), or if you are pressed for time, use ready-mades as a backdrop for your creative embroidery ideas. The embroidery techniques will be the same for both.

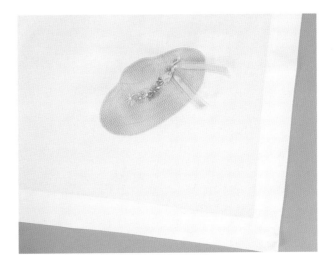

Use the ideas in the book to stimulate your own ideas for party decorations, and adapt the techniques to suit your tastes. For instance, the Tea in the Garden tablecloth was purchased and machine embroidered appliqués were stitched in the corners. You could easily make your own tablecloth with the appliqués if you prefer. The reverse is also possible. The place mats in the Fairy Gathering are made with coordinating fabrics, but you may find ready-made place mats that will work just as well. The embroidery would be placed in the same corner on the place mat as with the handmade one. Using ready-made items can ease the pressure and still give your party an individual and creative flair.

Sizing for Tablecloths and Napkins

To find the appropriate size tablecloth, measure the length and width of your table. The amount of fabric on the sides of the table (the drop) is usually about 6"-12". For rectangular and square tables, add double the drop measurement to both the length and the width. For example, a 40" x 60" table with a 10" drop would need a 60" x 80" tablecloth. For a round table, add double the desired drop to the diameter of the table. Most round tables are 30" high. If you want the drop to go to the floor, add 60" to the diameter.

If you are making your own tablecloth, add enough fabric for the hems as well. Fabrics are usually 42"-45" or 54" wide, which means that most tablecloths must be pieced. It is best to put the seam along the side of the table, not directly on top of it. For a 60" x 80" tablecloth with 2" hems on all sides, the new size would be 64" x 84". You will need two lengths of 45" fabric that are 84" long. One 45" x 84" piece is for the top. The second piece will be cut into two 10½" x 84" pieces (add two inches for ½" seam allowances). The seams would be along the sides and not on the top of the table.

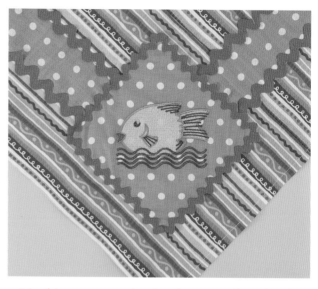

Napkins can vary in size from small cocktail to large dinner-size napkins. Cocktail napkins are usually about 12" or 13", while the large dinner napkins can be 20" to 22". You can decide how big to make your own. If you want to use a fat quarter of fabric, make your napkins 17" square. I have given measurements for each project, but you can make your napkins whatever size fits your needs.

Embroidery Designs as Appliqués and Stand-alone Projects

Most of us think machine-embroidered designs must be stitched on the surface of clothing or linens, but they can also be used alone for a variety of projects. The designs must be stitched to a fabric or stabilizer and then cut out very close to the edges. There are several methods to make these stand-alone designs.

1 If the design has many angles around the edge, such as the Zinnia in the Day at the Beach, stitch it onto several layers of nylon organza. Cut close to the edges with a sharp scissors. Use a hot knife or hot textile tool to melt the edges close to the embroidery.

4 Metallic threads may not work as well when stitched on stabilizer only, or if your design has some of the background showing, such as the Mardi Gras! Large Mask. In these cases, use fabric over the stabilizer in the hoop. After the design is stitched, apply a seam sealant close to the outline and let it dry before cutting. This ensures that there will be no fraying fabric threads from the background showing.

Metallic Threads

Many sewers are shy about using metallic threads because they are more difficult to work with, but these three tips for using metallic threads will help you achieve great results.

1 Always use a metallic embroidery needle. I have better results with a size 90 needle.

2 Lower the thread tension on your machine. Experiment with each thread to see which setting works the best.

3 If you are stitching a narrow satin stitch outline, or other area where the machine is stitching very quickly, slow down the speed of your machine.

2 Use heavy cut-away stabilizer in the hoop and stitch the design. Test the design with one or two layers to see which will work the best for your threads and machine. If it turns out well the first time, you can use it as is! Cut as closely as possible to the edge of the design with a very sharp scissors. If some of the stabilizer still shows, touch it up with a permanent marker the same color as the thread. Some of the designs have tiny stitched components, such as the Butterfly antennae in the Fairy Gathering. In this case, I simply cut about 1/6" beyond the embroidery, leaving the stabilizer showing around all the edges.

3 Embroidery designs can be stitched on several layers of a water-soluble stabilizer. Then, remove the design from the hoop and cut the stabilizer close to the design. Rinse the motif in warm water to wash away any remaining stabilizer. Let dry before using it.

Birthday Bash

Everyone deserves to have a fabulous party on his or her special day! Create lasting decorations for your family by combining colorful party fabrics and festive embroidery designs. A tablecloth, embroidered place mats, place card holders and a unique birthday bouquet will make every birthday party a joyful celebration.

Party Hat Place Card

These hats are made with cheery party fabric over heavy interfacing.

The double cord trim is glued in a spiral fashion and will hold a place card.

The card has been decorated with the Balloon embroidery design,

but the strings have been eliminated.

Supplies for one place card holder:

13" x 8" piece of fabric

13" x 8" piece of heavy fusible interfacing

1 yd. each narrow cord in two colors

15" pompom fringe (pompoms are ½")

Curly ribbon from a package bow (for the top of the hat)

3" lightweight wire

Fabric glue

Balloon embroidery design

Cut-away stabilizer

40-wt. embroidery thread

1½" x 3" piece of white card stock

1¾" x 3¼" piece of colored card stock

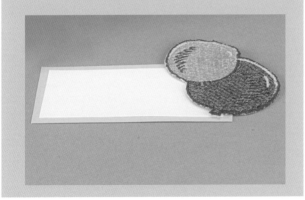

Directions:

1 Cut one hat from fabric using the pattern piece on pg. 15. Cut one hat from the interfacing following the interfacing cutting line at the lower edge.

2 Place the interfacing on the wrong side of the fabric and fuse, following manufacturer's instructions. Be sure that the hat extends ½" below the interfacing at the lower edge. Fold the fabric at the lower edge ½" over the interfacing and stitch.

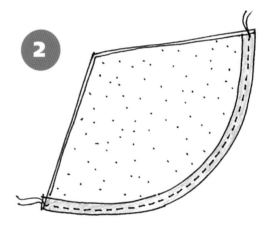

3 Pin the two cords to the top of the hat at the point so the ends will be caught in the seam line. With right sides together, sew the side edges. Press the seam allowances open and turn to the right side.

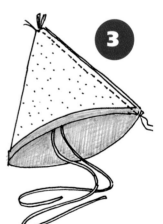

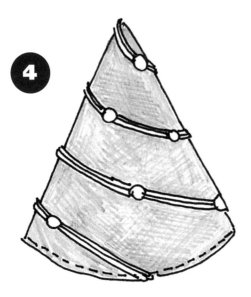

4 Wrap the two cords around the outside of the hat in a spiral fashion. Use fabric glue at approximately 3" intervals around the hat to secure. Turn the cords under the hat when you reach the bottom edge. Stitch the ends in place.

5 Place the heading of the pompom fringe under the lower edge and stitch, overlapping the ends.

6 Cut 6-8 ribbon curls about 4" long from the package bow, and tie together at one end with the wire, leaving about 1" straight at the end of the wire. Put glue at the end of the wire, and poke it through the top of the hat.

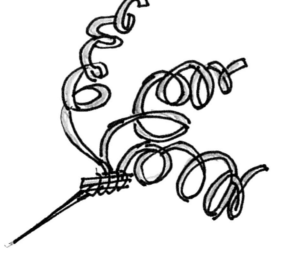

For the place card:

1 Hoop one or two pieces of stabilizer and stitch the Balloon design, eliminating the steps for the strings.

2 Remove from stabilizer, and cut as close to the edge as possible.

3 Glue the white card to the colored card. Glue the embroidery to the right side of the place card.

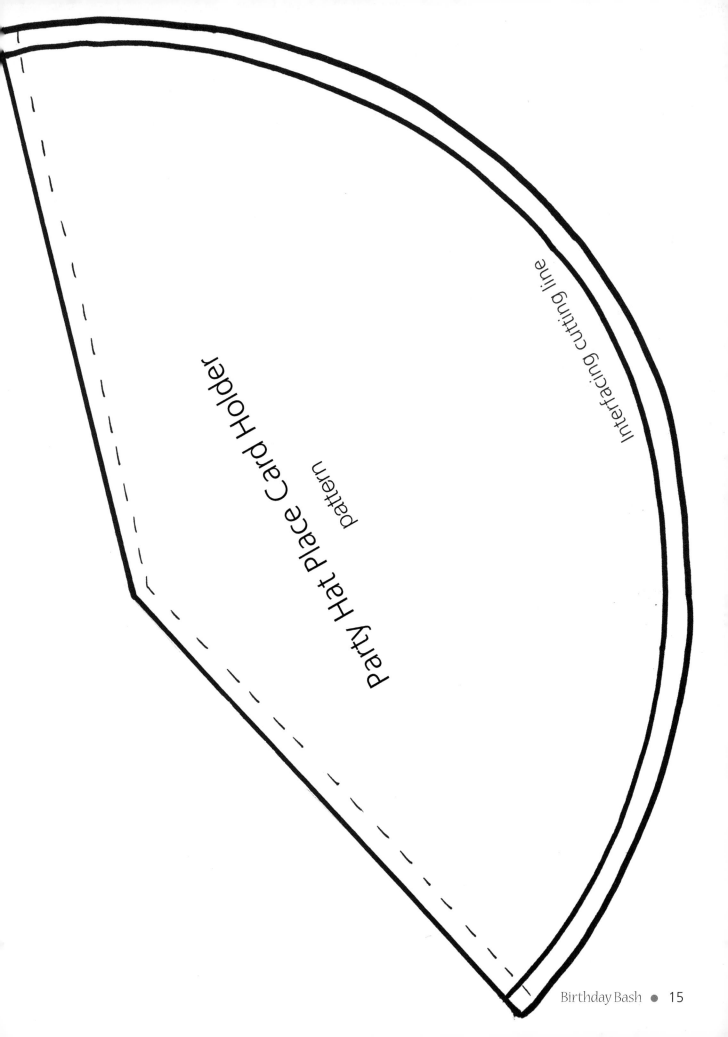

Party Hat Place Card Holder pattern

Interfacing cutting line

Place Mat of Honor

The Birthday Boy or Girl will love this place mat!
The simple patchwork design has embroidery stitched on the solid color patches.
Pompom fringe and two bright prints are
perfect finishing touches.

Supplies:

½ yd. solid color cotton fabric

¼ yd. print fabric

2 pieces contrasting print fabric, 3" x 15" each

Present, Happy Birthday and Cake embroidery designs

40-wt. embroidery thread

Tear-away stabilizer

1 yd. pompom fringe (pompoms are ½")

Fusible medium-weight interfacing

Directions:

1 Cut a 15" x 20" piece of the solid color fabric for the back of the place mat and set aside.

2 Cut the remaining solid color fabric into five pieces large enough to fit in the embroidery hoop. Hoop each one with stabilizer and embroider two Cakes, two Presents, and one Happy Birthday design. Remove from the hoop, and tear away the stabilizer. Cut each one into a 5½" square with the embroidery centered inside.

3 Cut four 5½" squares of the print fabric. With right sides together and a ½" seam allowance, sew the bottom edge of the square with a Present design to a print square, then the top edge of a square with a Cake to the other side of the print square. Repeat with a square with Cake, a print square, and then a square with Present. Sew the remaining two print squares to the top and the bottom of the square with Happy Birthday. Press seam allowances open.

4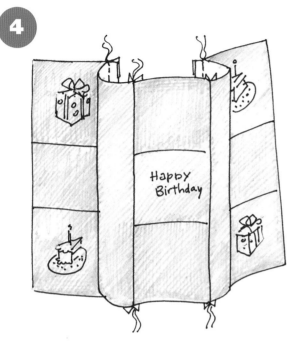

4 Using ½" seam allowances, sew the long strip of contrasting print fabric to the right side edge of the strip with the Present at the top. Sew the other side of the strip to the left side of the Happy Birthday strip. Sew the remaining side of the Happy Birthday strip to the other long strip of contrasting print fabric. Sew the remaining side of the long strip to the strip with the Cake at the top. Press seam allowances open.

5 Cut the interfacing to fit the place mat along the seam lines so that ½" of fabric extends beyond the interfacing on all sides. Fuse to the wrong side of the place mat, following manufacturer's instructions.

6 Press all the edges of the place mat ½" to the wrong side. Press all the edges of the place mat back ½" to the wrong side. Place them with wrong sides together, and topstitch ¼" from the pressed edges, placing the pompom fringe inside the side edges before stitching.

6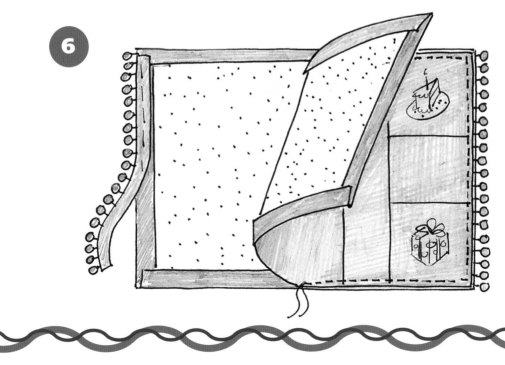

Guest Place Mat

All of your guests can have celebratory place mats, too!

Make these fun favors from a bright cotton print with three embroidered patches.

Don't forget the pompom fringe along one side!

Supplies for one place mat:

2 pieces of fabric, 14" x 20"

Light contrasting fabric for patches, large enough to hoop two times

Dark contrasting fabric for patches, large enough to hoop once

40-wt. embroidery thread

Balloons, Party Hat with Star and Party Hat with Stripes embroidery designs

Tear-away stabilizer

14" pompom fringe (pompoms are ½")

Fusible medium-weight interfacing

Directions:

1 Place the dark fabric with stabilizer in the hoop and embroider the Balloons design. Place the light fabric in the hoop with stabilizer and embroider one of the Party Hat designs. Repeat with the remaining piece of light fabric, and embroider the other Party Hat design.

2 Cut each of the embroidered fabrics in patches. Make the Balloons patch 4" wide x 5" high with the embroidery centered, make the Party Hat with Stripes 4" wide x 5" high with the design 1¼" from the bottom, and make the other Party Hat patch 4" wide x 5" high with the design 1¼" from the top.

3 Sew the patches with right sides together along the 4" edges using a ¼" seam allowance. The Party Hat with Star is first, the Balloons next, and the Party Hat with Stripes below. Press seam allowances open. Press the long sides ¼" to the wrong side.

4 Cut the interfacing 13" x 19" and fuse to the wrong side of one of the place mat pieces, following the manufacturer's instructions. Press all the sides ½" to the wrong side. Press the sides of the other place mat piece ½" to the wrong side.

5 Place the embroidered strip on the interfaced place mat 3" from the left side edge. Place the pompom fringe underneath the outer edge of the strip and stitch close to the edge. Stitch the other side of the strip close to the edge. Fold the top and bottom of the strip to the wrong side, flush with the place mat edges, and press.

6 Pin the place mats with wrong sides together and stitch around all sides.

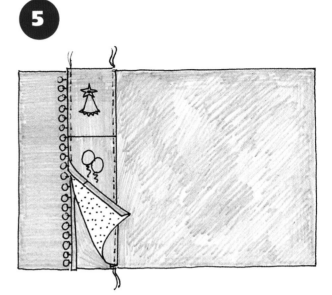

Napkins and Napkin Rings

These napkins are simply squares of fabric with hemmed edges.
Make them as large as you like. To vary the napkin rings, use the Party Hat with Stripes
or the Present as well as the Party Hat with Star embroidery design.

Supplies for one napkin and napkin ring:

18"-20" square of cotton fabric

Party Hat with Star embroidery design

Heavy cut-away stabilizer

40-wt. thread for Party Hat with Star design

3½" x 8" piece of orange fabric

1¼" x 7½" piece of fusible medium-weight or heavyweight interfacing

Fabric glue

Napkin:

1 Serge, zigzag stitch or pink around the edge of each napkin.

2 Press each edge of the napkin ½" to the wrong side.

3 Topstitch around the edges of each napkin ⅜" from the pressed edge.

Napkin Ring:

1 Hoop one or two layers of heavy cut-away stabilizer, depending on your experience as you tested the design. Embroider one Party Hat for each napkin ring. Cut away the stabilizer close to the stitching outline.

2 Press both long edges of the napkin ring ¼" to the wrong side. Place the interfacing horizontally in one of the folds and fuse according to manufacturer's instructions. With right sides together, stitch the short ends ¼" from the edge.

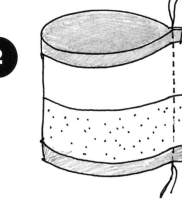

3 Press seam allowances open. Fold the napkin ring in half over the interfacing so that the pressed edges meet. Stitch close to the edge.

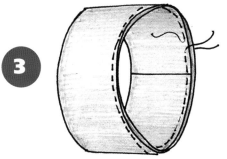

4 Glue the Party Hat to the napkin ring over the seam line.

Birthday Card

Make a unique card by stitching Happy Birthday embroidery designs on fabric.
Cut out the embroidered fabric with a scalloping or pinking shears,
and glue to folded card stock.

Supplies:

One sheet colored cardstock paper

Fabric large enough to fit in the
embroidery hoop

Tear away stabilizer

Happy Birthday embroidery design

40-wt. embroidery thread

¼ yd. ribbon, ¼ " wide

Fabric glue stick

Directions:

1 Place fabric in the hoop with the stabilizer, and embroider the design.

2 Remove the stabilizer and cut the fabric with scalloping or pinking shears so that it measures 3½" x 5".

3 Cut cardstock to measure 6" x 8½". Fold in half so that the card measures 6" x 4¼". Glue the embroidered fabric to the front of the card, centering the design.

4 Tie the ribbon into a bow. Tack with glue to the top of the embroidery in the center.

Other Ideas:

1 Stitch the outline of the Present directly on cardstock for a quick birthday card.

2 Use the Balloons design to decorate children's clothing.

3 Embroider the Party Hat designs to napkins for each family member, along with their names and birth dates.

4 Make a first birthday bib using the Cake design along with the name and date.

- *All threads in this section are Aurifil threads.*

- *All printed fabrics used in this section are from Camelot Cottons.*

- *Pompom fringe used in this section is from CheepTrims.com.*

BONUS PROJECT on CD: Balloon Bouquet

Tea in the Garden

Spring is a wonderful time to enjoy tea with your friends in the garden, so decorate for a leisurely event in either your dining room or a sun-drenched backyard patio. Use these flower-filled projects, your best china and lots of blossoms. You can also change the embroidery design colors to host a Red Hat Society party.

Straw Hat Tablecloth

A purchased square white cloth is the perfect palette for appliqué and embroidery!
First, embroider the straw hat appliqués with the Garland design, which acts as a hat band.
Then, fuse it to the tablecloth and stitch around the edges. If you do spill a little tea,
remove the bows on the appliqué before laundering.

Supplies for appliques in all four corners:

Purchased square tablecloth
  (cloth used was 52" x 52")

¼ yd. tan cotton fabric

Matching or contrasting color
  sewing thread

Fusible web

Garland embroidery design

Tear-away stabilizer

40-wt. embroidery thread

1⅓ yd. ribbon, ⅝" wide

Directions:

1 Cut four pieces of fabric large enough to fit the pattern piece on pg. 30 and also to fit in the hoop. Hoop one of them with stabilizer and stitch the design in the center. Remove from the hoop and tear away the stabilizer.

2 Place the pattern piece on the fabric so that the garland is properly aligned, and cut it out. Place a piece of fusible web with the sticky side down over the right side of the fabric. Stitch around the appliqué on the seam line. Trim the seam allowance and make a slit in the fusible web. Turn the fabric to the right side and finger press around the edges.

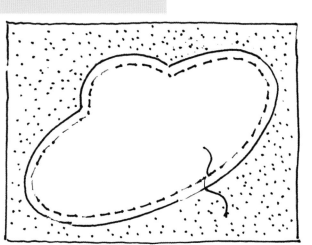

3 Place the appliqué on the corner and press into place. (For a 52" square cloth, the appliqué is 9" from the point.) Using a 1.5 width and a 0.6 length stitch and the sewing thread, stitch the detail lines in the hat. Increase the width to 2.5 and stitch around the outside.

4 Cut the ribbon into four pieces and tie one of them into a bow. Tack the bow to the right side of the garland.

5 Repeat steps 1-4 with remaining supplies for the three remaining corners.

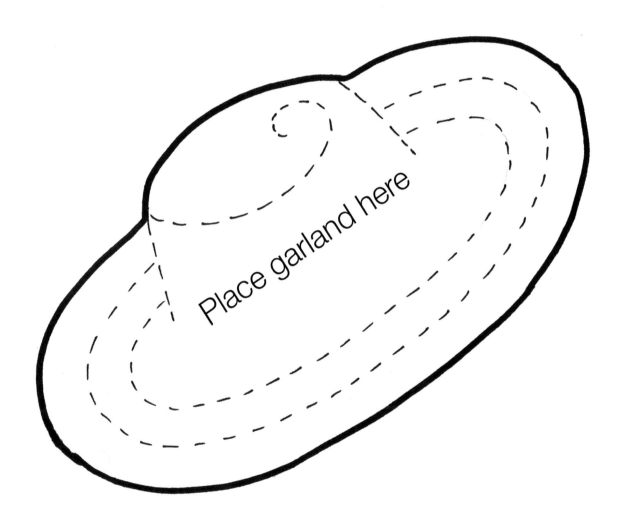

Place garland here

Fete Favor

*Purses are fun accessories, and your guests will love these miniature versions
filled with sweets, flower seeds or other goodies. The bag has a flat bottom
so it will stand upright on the table and welcome your friends to the party.*

Supplies for one favor:

¼ yd. cotton fabric

Small Bouquet embroidery design

40-wt. embroidery thread

Tear-away stabilizer

⅓ yd. double-faced satin ribbon, ¼" wide

Small snap

Scrap of cardstock paper

Directions:

1 Hoop a piece of fabric and stabilizer large enough for the purse front. Embroider the design; remove the hoop and remove the stabilizer.

2 Trace the purse pattern on the embroidered fabric so that the embroidery is centered. Cut out the front and cut another one for the back. Cut out one purse bottom.

3 With right sides together and ¼" seam allowances, sew the purse from the front to the back along one of the side seams. Press the seam allowances open. Press the top edge of the purse ¼" to the wrong side and topstitch.

4 Pin both sides of the purse bottom to the bottom edge of the purse with right sides together. The open sides of the purse will meet at one point of the purse bottom. Stitch with a ¼" seam allowance. Press the seam allowances to one side.

5 Stitch the remaining side seam with a ¼" seam allowance. Press seam allowances open.

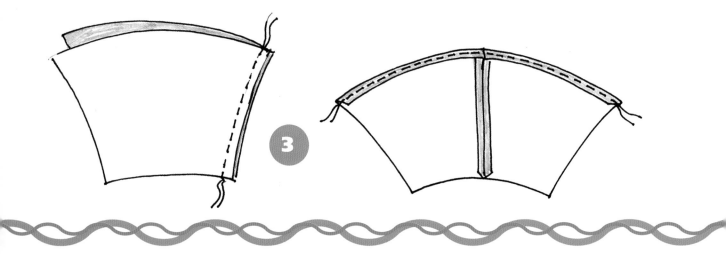

6 Cut the ribbon into two 5½" pieces. Sew both ends of one piece 1" from the center of the top edge of the purse front. Repeat with the back of the purse. Sew a snap to the top edge at the center.

7 If desired, cut a piece of cardstock to fit the bottom of the purse to add stability.

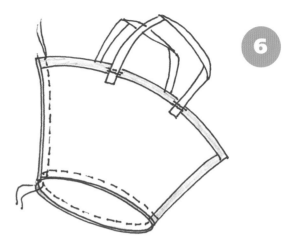

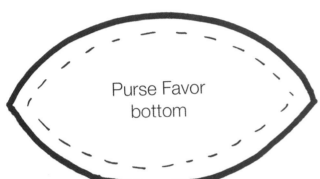

Purse Favor bottom

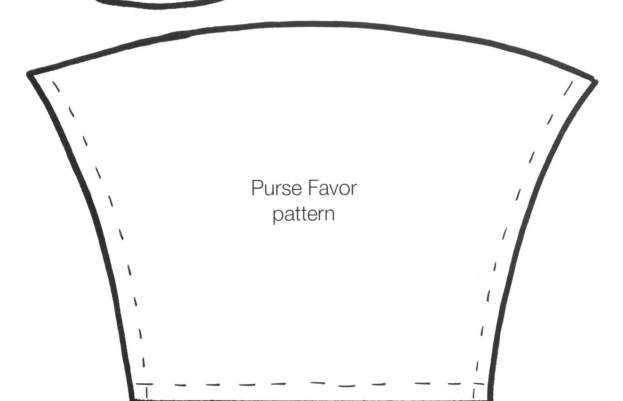

Purse Favor pattern

Tea Cozy

What would a tea party be without a beautiful teapot?
Dress up your favorite teapot with this lovely tea cozy. It has insulated batting
and ties around the spout to keep your tea toasty. Match the flower colors
in the design to the posies on your table.

Supplies:

¼ yd. cotton fabric

2 pieces of insulated batting 6" x 11", such as Insul-Bright

Large Bouquet embroidery design

40-wt. embroidery thread

Tear-away stabilizer

Temporary spray adhesive

2⅔ yd. ribbon, ¼" wide

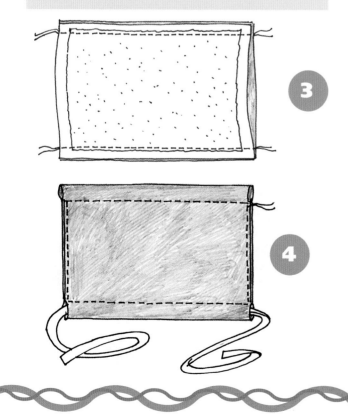

Directions:

1 Cut four pieces of fabric 7" high x 11" wide. Place one of the pieces into the hoop with stabilizer. Center the embroidery design and stitch. Remove from the hoop and tear away the stabilizer.

2 Spray the batting side of the insulated batting with the temporary spray adhesive. Place the insulated batting on the wrong side of the embroidered fabric so that the fabric extends ½" beyond the batting on each side edge. Baste along the top and bottom edges ½" from the edge. Trim the batting close to the stitching to eliminate bulk.

3 With right sides together, sew the embroidered fabric to another piece of the fabric along the top and bottom edges with a ½" seam allowance. Turn to the right side and press.

4 Fold the side edges of the tea cozy ½" to the wrong side and stitch close to the folded edges, leaving ½" open at the top and bottom of the seams. Make a casing along the top and bottom edges by stitching ½" away from the edge.

5 Repeat steps 2, 3 and 4 with the remaining two pieces of fabric and the insulated batting.

6 Cut the ribbon into four pieces and thread one piece through each of the casings. Tie around a tea pot so that the handle and the spout protrude between the two sections.

Hostess Apron

June Cleaver will be jealous when you wear this charming apron.

You can choose any apron pattern and embroider the Tea Pot design on the pocket.

Add a ruffle with contrasting piping — and don't forget to wear your pearls!

Supplies:

Apron pattern of your choice

Green checked fabric (see pattern instructions for yardage)

Grosgrain ribbon for ties (see pattern instructions for yardage)

Teapot embroidery design

Tear-away stabilizer

40-wt. embroidery thread

Lace edging to go around the pocket, sides and bottom edges

1 package pre-made piping

Directions:

1 Cut out apron using the pattern pieces.

2 Cut a piece for the pocket that is large enough to fit in the hoop and that will accommodate the pocket pattern piece. Hoop the fabric and the stabilizer, and embroider the design. Remove from the hoop and tear away the stabilizer. Press.

3 Cut out the pocket, centering the embroidery design. Cut another pocket from the fabric for the lining. Cut a piece of piping long enough to go around the pocket sides and bottom edge, plus ¼" at each end. Stitch the piping and then the lace edging to the seam line of the side and bottom edges of the embroidered pocket, turning the raw ends.

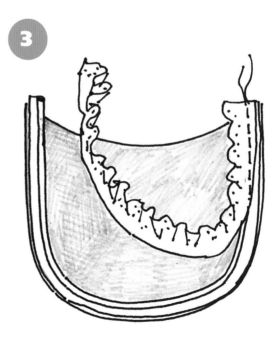

4

4 Stitch the lining to the pocket with right sides together along the curved edge. Clip the curves; trim the seam, and turn to the right side. Press. Fold the top edges of the pocket to the inside and topstitch.

5 Stitch the pocket where indicated on the apron. Continue assembly of the apron according to the pattern instructions. Place the piping and then the lace edging around the side and bottom edges before sewing the lining to the apron.

Other Ideas:

1 The Large Bouquet design can be stitched in pastels or shades of white and cream to be used for wedding projects, such as a guest book cover or table linens.

2 The Small Bouquet design can be stitched in the bridal party colors and placed on shower invitations or napkins. It can also be stitched on small potpourri bags for favors.

3 The Teapot design can be stitched on kitchen towels or pot holders. Stitch them in a row for a small curtain valance.

4 The Straw Hat design can be embroidered, cut out, and placed on an invitation.

• *Apron pattern used was "Newfangled Reversible Aprons" by Mary Mulari, Mary's Productions.*

• *All threads shown on the projects are Madeira USA embroidery threads.*

**BONUS PROJECTS on CD:
Napkins and Napkin Rings**

Game Night

Whether you host a weekly card party or
an occasional game night with friends,
this group of game supplies will add
to the festivities. The green felt mat is
sized for a card table, but you can use
it anywhere you want to play. Decorate
the coasters and tally card holders with
only one suit so players can keep track
of their own. The Party Box is perfect for
holding all your game supplies — just
add the food and the fun!

Party Box

This box, purchased at a craft store, is just the right size for cards, dice and chips.

Simply cut out the designs and glue!

Supplies:

Box for holding cards, chips and dice

Joker Hat and Four Suits embroidery designs

Heavy cut-away stabilizer

40-wt. embroidery thread

Fast-drying glue

Directions:

1 Place one or two pieces of stabilizer in the embroidery hoop, and stitch the Joker Hat design. Remove from the hoop, and cut carefully around the edges with a sharp scissors.

2 Place one or two pieces of stabilizer in the embroidery hoop, and stitch the Four Suits design. Remove from the hoop, and cut carefully around the edges of each shape with a sharp scissors. You will now have four separate designs.

3 Glue the Joker Hat to the top of the box, and attach each of the Four Suits to the front of the box (see photo for placement).

Four-Suit Coasters

Make a different coaster for each player using the four suits.
Use wool or craft-quality felt — both will give good results.

Supplies for one red suit and one black suit coaster:

¼ yd. red wool or craft felt

¼ yd. black wool or craft felt

Individual Red Suit and Black Suit embroidery designs

40-wt. embroidery thread

Triangle pattern

Square pattern

Directions:

1 Cut pieces of both red and black felt large enough to fit in the hoop. Stitch a Red Suit design on the red felt and a Black Suit design on the black felt. Remove from the hoop and press.

2 For the Red Suit design coaster, cut out a triangle for the top of the coaster from the plain black felt using the pattern piece on pg. 46. Cut the same triangle from the Red Suit embroidered felt. Cut a square from red felt using the pattern piece on pg. 46.

3 Place the embroidered triangle and a plain black triangle on a red square. The diagonal edges of the triangles should meet. Stitch around the triangles with matching thread very close to the edges, including the diagonal edges.

4 For the Black Suit design coaster, cut out a triangle for the top of the coaster using the pattern piece from the plain red felt. Cut the same triangle from the Black Suit embroidered felt. Cut a square from black felt using the pattern piece.

5 Place the black embroidered triangle and a plain red triangle on a black square. The diagonal edges of the triangles should meet. Stitch around the triangles with matching thread very close to the edges, including the diagonal edges.

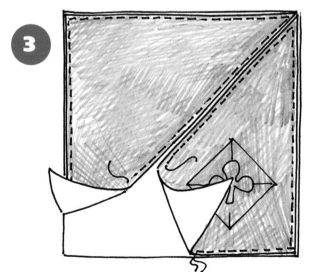

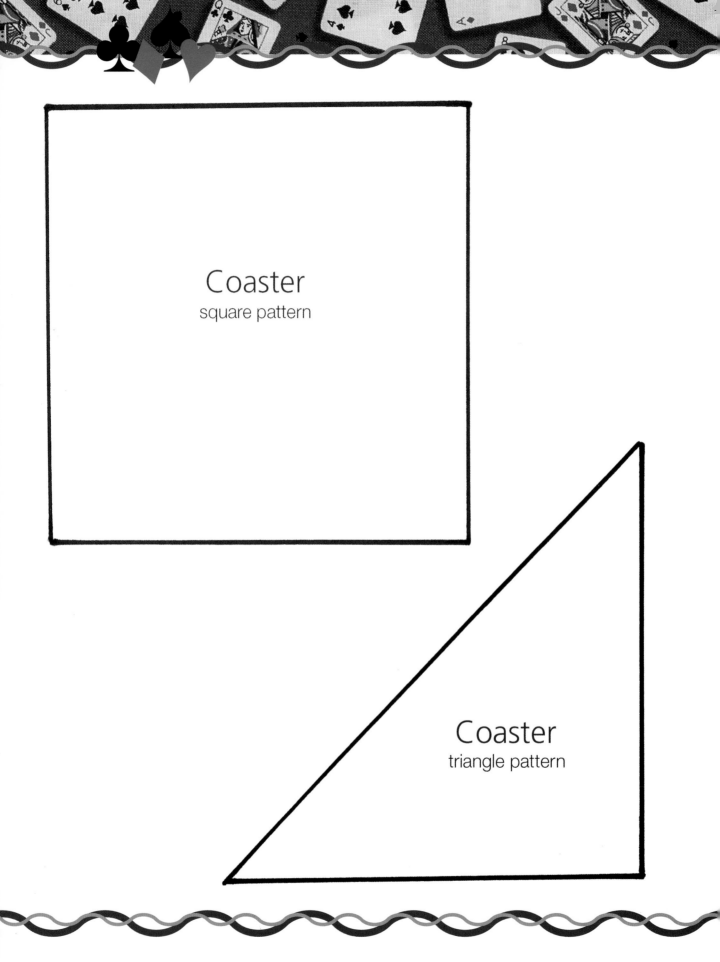

Coaster
square pattern

Coaster
triangle pattern

Tally Card Holder

Make game night even more fun with tally card holders
embroidered to match the coasters — just glue the front of the card
to the inside of the holder. If you glue carefully, you can reuse the cardholder.

Supplies for one red suit and one black suit card holders:

Red and black wool or craft felt large enough to fit in the hoop, approximately 6" square

Individual Red Suit and Black Suit embroidery designs

40-wt. embroidery thread

Tally cards

Fabric glue

Directions:

1 Place the red felt in the hoop and embroider a Red Suit design. Make sure you have 2-¾" of felt to the left of the design for the holder. Place the black felt in the hoop and embroider a Black Suit design, making sure that you have 2-¾" of felt to the left of the design. Remove from the hoop and press.

2 Cut each cardholder 4" wide x 4-¾" high. The embroidery should be centered from top to bottom and placed ¼" from the right-side edge. Fold in half lengthwise.

3 Glue the top of the tally card to the inside of the holder.

Score Pad Holder

*This felt holder has a pocket on the inside to hold a score pad.
Use only the center suits from the Four Suit embroidery design
so you won't have to worry about lining up the designs.*

Supplies:

Red wool or craft felt, 4" wide x 15½" long

Four Suits embroidery design

Adhesive stabilizer

40-wt. embroidery thread

Score pad

Directions:

1 Hoop the stabilizer and remove the paper on the top. Baste the design outline on the stabilizer without any thread or fabric to find the outline of the design in the hoop. Mark the spot on the felt for the embroidery design. The first Suit motif, centered widthwise, begins 10¾" from the top edge and ends 1" from the bottom edge. Place the felt over the stabilizer so the design will be in the right place.

2 Stitch the two center shapes from the Four Suits design, following steps #5-12 in the embroidery design only. Remove from the stabilizer and press.

3 Measure 4" from the top edge and press the felt to wrong side along this line. Stitch closely to each edge to create a pocket.

4 Measure 6" from the bottom edge and fold over the pocket. Press along this line.

5 Insert the cardboard pad from the back of the score pad holder into the pocket.

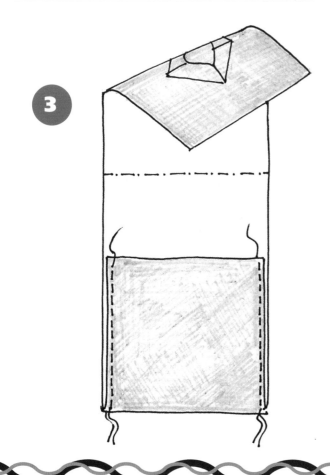

Other Ideas:

1 Stitch a row of the Individual Diamond Suits for a classic look on a jacket or pillow.

2 Isolate the outline of the heart, spade, club or diamond shapes from the Individual Suits to use for an invitation.

• *All threads used in these projects are by Robison-Anton.*

BONUS PROJECTS on CD:
Card Table Mat and Napkins

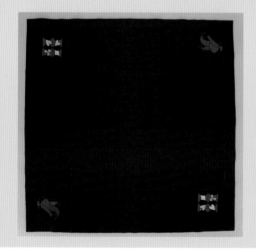

Day at the Beach

Your Beach Party bash will be the talk of the town with all of your own embroidered decorations. Bright, summery stripes and polka dots with embroidery and rickrack are a winning combination — just add tiki torches, cool drinks and a picnic basket!

Weighted Tablecloth

*The embroidered pocket at each corner of this 96" x 54" tablecloth contains
a drapery weight to keep the cloth from blowing away in the breeze. Take the weights out before laundering the tablecloth. This tablecloth has been sized to fit a 6' picnic table, so make the appropriate adjustments if you have a different-sized table.*

Supplies:

5⅓ yd. fabric, 45" wide

17 yd. jumbo rickrack

2⅓ yd. medium rickrack

½ yd. contrasting fabric for borders and pockets

4 fabric-covered drapery weights

40-wt. embroidery thread

Tear-away stabilizer

Fish and Umbrella embroidery designs

4 large snaps

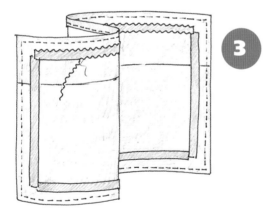

Directions:

1 Cut the tablecloth fabric to make two 97" panels. Cut one of the panels lengthwise so that one of the sections measures 10" x 97". Sew right sides together to make the tablecloth 55" x 97". Press seam allowances to one side. Serge, zigzag stitch or pink around all edges of the tablecloth. Press edges ½" to the wrong side, and stitch.

2 Cut contrasting fabric into five 2" x 45"-wide strips. Piece together to make two 89"-long strips and two 48"-long strips.

3 Place the strips on the tablecloth 3" from the finished edge (the ends can overlap because they will be covered by the embroidered patches). Place the jumbo rickrack over each strip edge, and stitch.

4 Cut four pieces of fabric large enough to fit in the hoop. Hoop two of them with stabilizer, and embroider the Fish design. Hoop the remaining two pieces with stabilizer, and embroider the Umbrella design. Cut them into 5½" diamond shapes, centering the embroidery design. Place the medium rickrack on the outside edge of each embroidered patch, and stitch.

5 Center each patch in the corners of the tablecloth. Stitch over the previous stitching on the rickrack, leaving 1½" open on each side of the point at the top. Place a drapery weight inside each patch. Sew snaps to the point of the patches and the tablecloth.

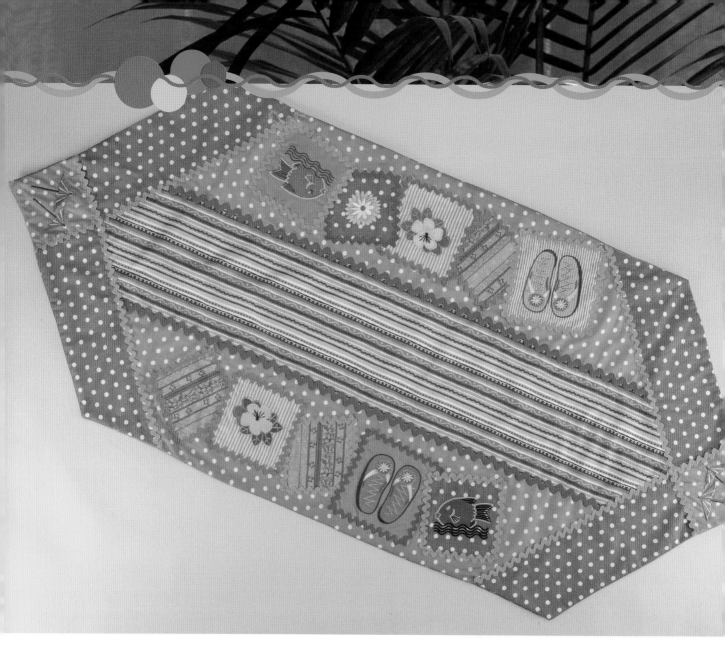

Colorful Table Runner

This festive runner is the perfect colorful focal point of your table.
It includes many embroidery designs along with the striped and polka dot fabrics,
and the cotton flannel filling gives it a slight loft.

Supplies:

7½" x 38" piece of striped fabric

1½ yd. primary color polka dot fabric

⅓ yd. secondary color polka dot fabric

Scraps of solid color, print or polka dot fabric for embroidered patches

2 yd. jumbo rickrack

2¼ yd. primary color medium rickrack

Assorted colors of medium rickrack for patches

Hibiscus, Fish, Umbrella, Zinnia and Flip-flop embroidery designs

Tear-away stabilizer

40-wt. embroidery thread

Fusible interfacing

1½ yd. pastel colored flannel

Directions:

Note: all seam allowances are ¼".

1 Cut two pieces of the primary color polka dot fabric to fit in the hoop. Hoop both pieces with stabilizer, and stitch the Umbrella design in both. Remove from the hoop, and press. Cut the embroidered pieces in a 5" diamond shape.

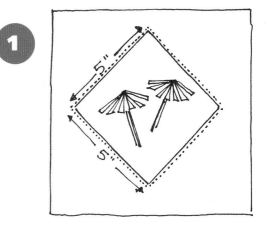

2 Embroider two Flip-flops, two Fish, two Hibiscus and one Zinnia on the fabric of your choice, using the method described above. Cut the Flip-flop pieces into 5½" squares, the Fish and the Hibiscus pieces into 4½" squares and the Zinnia piece into a 4" square. Cut three more patches into 4" squares from the remaining scrap fabric for the patches.

3 Cut two pieces of primary color polka dot fabric 7½" x 38". With right sides together, sew one long side of the polka dot pieces to one long side of the striped fabric. Sew the other polka dot piece to the other side of the striped fabric. Press seam allowances open.

4

4 Cut four pieces of secondary polka dot fabric 5" x 14". With right sides together, stitch one side of the polka dot fabric to the upper right side of the Umbrella diamond. Sew another polka dot piece to the upper left side of the Umbrella diamond. Press seam allowances open.

5 Press the inside edge of the polka dot/diamond piece ¼" to the wrong side, making a clip at the corner. Place this pressed edge over the striped fabric combo so that the inner corner of the polka dot/diamond piece is ¼" from the edge in the center of the striped fabric combo, and topstitch. On the wrong side, trim away the excess striped fabric combo along the seam allowances. Trim the side edges of the polka dot/diamond piece so they are flush with the side edges of the striped fabric combo. Repeat with the polka dot/diamond piece at the other end.

6 Sew the jumbo rickrack over the center seams of the runner. Sew the primary color medium rickrack along the seam lines at each end between the polka dot/diamond and the striped fabric combo.

5

7 Arrange the patches on each side of the runner, placing one plain patch, a Flip-flop, Fish, Zinnia, and Hibiscus on one side, and two plain patches, a Flip-flop, Hibiscus and Fish on the other side. They should overlap at the corners as shown in the photo.

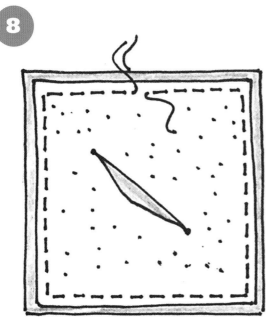

8 Cut a piece of fusible interfacing to fit each patch. With the right side of the fabric to the fusible side of the interfacing, sew around all of the edges of the patches. Cut a slit in the interfacing. Turn to the right side, and finger press flat. Fuse each one to the table runner, following the manufacturer's instructions. Sew rickrack around all the edges of the patches, turning the end under when you have finished.

9 Cut a piece of flannel and a piece of the primary polka dot fabric the same size as the table runner. Place the flannel over the wrong side of the backing, and baste around the edges. With right sides together, sew the table runner top to the back, leaving an opening for turning. Clip the corners; turn to the right side, and press. Stitch the opening closed.

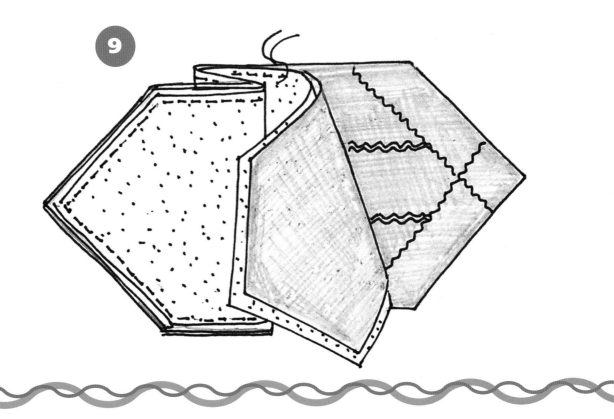

Funky Flip-flops

Wear a fancy pair of flip-flops decorated with rickrack,
trims and embroidered zinnias to your party, or make them for your guests
as a creative party favor. My daughter wants to wear them, so I can guarantee
they are daughter-approved!

Supplies:

One pair flip-flops

1 yd. jumbo rickrack

1 yd. trim, ¼" wide

Beacon Flip-flop Glue,
   or other firm-hold glue

Zinnia embroidery design

Nylon organza

40-wt. embroidery thread

Hot knife or hot textile tool

Directions:

1 Hoop two or three layers of organza. Embroider the Zinnia design twice, and remove from the hoop. Cut closely around the design. Use the hot knife or the hot textile tool to melt the remaining nylon fibers.

2 Cut the rickrack and trim so that it will fit each side of the strap. Glue the rickrack first and then the trim.

3 Glue one Zinnia embroidery design to the center of the straps on each flip-flop.

Watermelon Tumbler Cover

Drinks will stay cold when you provide your guests with insulated covers for their glasses.
The batting inside the cover has a special surface to keep the cold in or out, depending on
the type of drink. The Velcro closure makes it easy to fit on the glass.

Supplies for one cover (will fit 3"-wide glass):

Two 8" squares of striped cotton fabric

¼ yd. polka dot fabric

1 yd. narrow rickrack

3½" strip Velcro

4½" x 10¼" piece of insulated batting, such as Insul-Bright

Watermelon embroidery design

Tear-away stabilizer

40-wt. embroidery thread

Directions:

Note: all seam allowances in this project are ¼".

1 Hoop one square of the striped fabric with the stabilizer, and embroider the Watermelon design in the center. Remove the stabilizer, and cut it to measure 3" high x 5¾" wide, centering the watermelon. Repeat with the remaining square of striped fabric.

2 With right sides together, sew the striped pieces along one of the short sides. The embroidered piece will now measure 3" x 10¾". Sew the narrow rickrack over the seam.

3 Cut two pieces of polka dot fabric 1¼" x 10¾". With right sides together, sew them to each long edge of the embroidered fabric. Press the seam allowances open. Sew the narrow rickrack over the two long seams, overlapping the edges of the rickrack in the center.

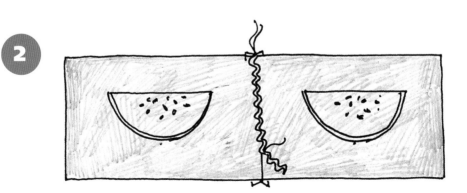

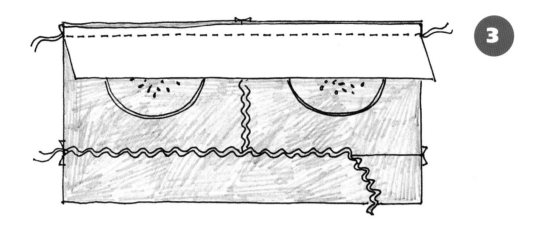

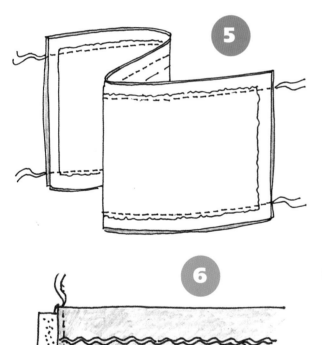

4 Cut a piece of polka dot fabric 4½" x 10¾". Place the insulating batting on the wrong side of the fabric so that the fabric extends ¼" beyond the edges of the batting. Baste the batting to the fabric, and trim the batting close to the seam line to reduce bulk.

5 With right sides together, sew the embroidered front to the fabric with batting along the long edges. Turn to the right side and press. Fold both of the short side edges ¼" to the inside, and topstitch.

6 Stitch the hook side of the Velcro under the right end so that it is flush with the fabric seam. Sew the loop side to the left end, so most of it extends beyond the fabric. Wrap the holder around the glass, and fasten it so that the side seams meet.

Fruit Slice Coaster

Garnish margaritas with embroidered fruit slices!

The embroidery design is worked on two sections placed on a solid bottom piece,

with the stem fitting between the two pieces of moisture-absorbing felt on the top.

Make several coasters with embroidered slices of oranges, lemons, limes or grapefruit

so that your guests will recognize their glasses.

Supplies for one coaster:

Wool felt, large enough to hoop twice, and a 5" square for the back of the coaster

Orange Slice or Watermelon embroidery design

40-wt. embroidery thread

Coaster pattern

Directions:

1 Place the wool felt in the hoop, and embroider the Orange Slice or Watermelon design. Place another piece of felt in the hoop and embroider a second design.

2 Cut the felt approximately ⅛" from the straight side of the design.

3 Cut a bottom for the coaster using the pattern piece on pg. 67. Place your stemware on the center of the felt bottom. Place the embroidered orange slices on two sides of the stem of the glass, and pin to the felt bottom. (This is a necessary step because stems can have different thicknesses.) Trace the outline of the glass felt bottom on the wrong side of the embroidered felt pieces, and cut along this line.

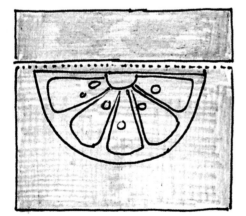

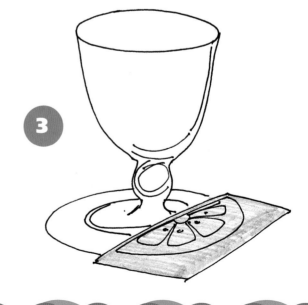

4 Stitch around the coaster ¼" from the edge with contrasting thread. Using a pinking or scalloping shears, cut close to the stitching around the coaster.

Fruit Slice
Coaster bottom pattern

Flip-flop Fork Holder

This clever utensil holder will hold flatware for each party guest.
Embroider with the Small Zinnia design before assembling,
and use a heavyweight interfacing inside to keep it sturdy.

Supplies for each holder:

¼ yd. fabric

Scraps of contrasting fabric for strap

¼ yd. heavyweight interfacing

Small Zinnia embroidery design

Tear-away stabilizer

40-wt. embroidery thread

Flip-flop pattern

Strap pattern

Directions:

1 Enlarge the Small Zinnia design by 20%.

2 Trace one flip-flop shape from the pattern piece on pg. 71 onto the fabric, but do not cut it. Cut out one strap from the contrasting fabric using the pattern piece on pg. 71. Spray the back of the strap with temporary spray adhesive, and place into position on the traced flip-flop. Stitch around the outside of the strap using a narrow zigzag stitch.

3 Place the traced flip-flop into the hoop with the stabilizer so that the top of the strap is centered. Embroider the Small Zinnia design. Remove from the hoop, tear away the stabilizer and cut out the flip-flop.

4 Cut out three more flip-flop shapes from the fabric, and cut two from the interfacing. Place the interfacing on the wrong side of the embroidered flip-flop, and stitch around the outer edge. Trim the interfacing close to the stitching. Repeat with another flip-flop section for the back.

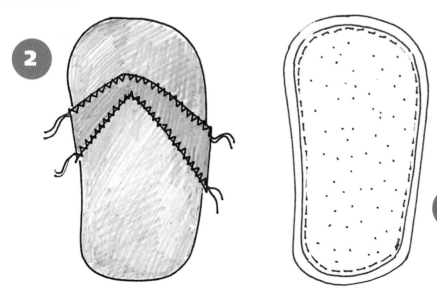

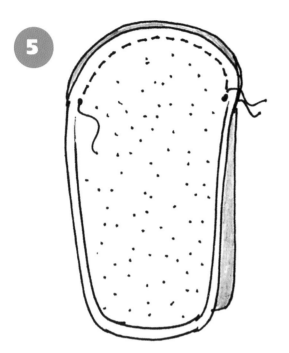

5 With right sides together and a ¼" seam allowance, sew the embroidered flip-flop to another along the top edge between the dots marked on the pattern piece. Repeat with the remaining two flip-flops for the back. Clip the curves; turn to the right side, and press. Baste the unstitched edges together.

6 Sew the flip-flops, right sides together, along the unfinished edges using a ¼" seam. Zigzag stitch or serge the edges to finish the seam allowances. Turn to the right side and press.

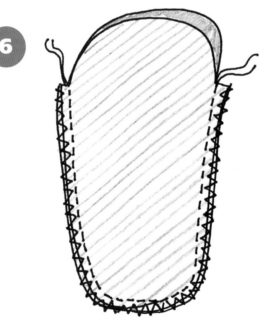

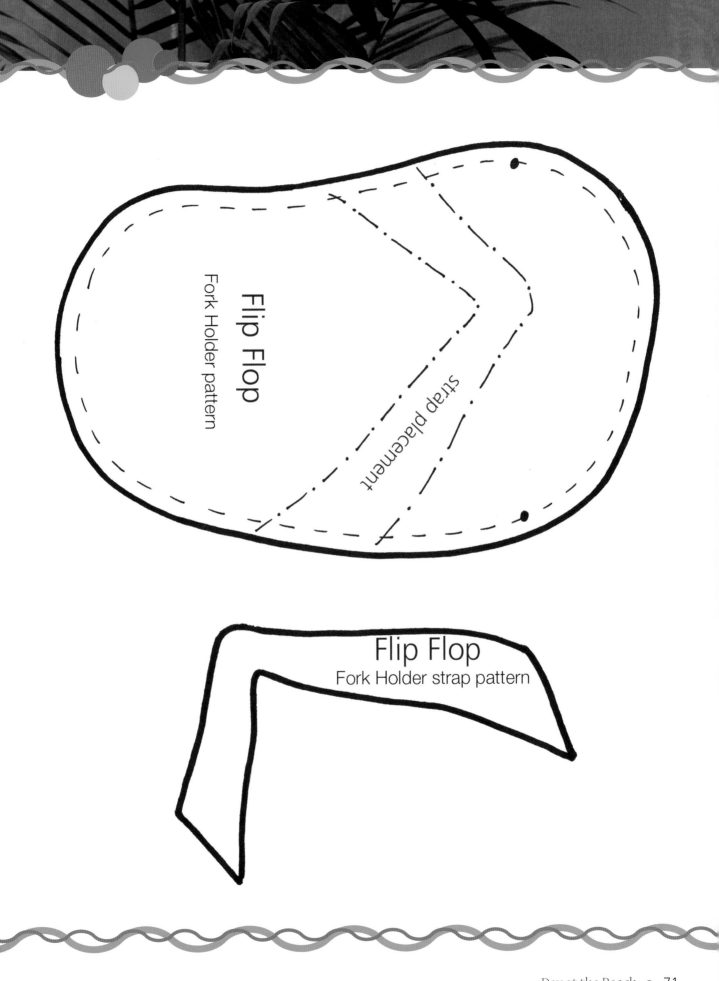

Flip Flop
Fork Holder pattern

strap placement

Flip Flop
Fork Holder strap pattern

Invitation

Guests will know they are in for a special treat when they receive this handmade invitation.
The sunglasses are made from a transparent plastic report cover found at office supply stores.

Supplies:

8½" x 11" piece of colored cardstock paper

8½" x 11" piece of white cardstock paper

Transparent colored report cover

Small Zinnia embroidery design

Water-soluble stabilizer

40-wt. embroidery thread

Jumbo rickrack

Glue stick

Glasses pattern

Directions:

1 Cut glasses shape from blue cardstock using the pattern piece below. Cut lenses from report cover using the pattern piece below. Glue the lenses to the back of the glasses and set aside.

2 Hoop two layers of water-soluble stabilizer, and embroider two Small Zinnias. Remove from hoop, and wash away the stabilizer according to manufacturer's instructions.

3 Fold the white cardstock in half widthwise. Glue rickrack to the card ¾" from the edge. Glue the glasses to the front at an angle. Glue the embroidered zinnias at each corner of the glasses.

4 Write a fun message on the front and party information inside!

Flower Drink Holder

Give each guest a holder decorated with a colorful embroidery design for frosty beverages.
Inexpensive plain foam drink holders can be purchased at most craft stores.

Supplies for one drink holder:

Drink holder

Embroidery design (pictured here: Orange Slice and Hibiscus)

40-wt. embroidery thread

Cut-away stabilizer

Fast-drying glue

Directions:

1 Hoop the stabilizer and stitch the desired design.

2 Cut close to the design, and glue to the side of the drink holder.

Other Ideas:

1 Stitch Zinnia designs in white, and glue them to the tops of flip-flops for the bride to wear at her wedding dance. Make several in the bridal party colors for the bridesmaids.

2 Use the Watermelon design in a tote bag, table runner or tablecloth as part of your 4th of July decorations.

3 Stitch the Fish design to a pair of bib overalls for a little boy or girl. The Fish can also decorate bathroom towels.

• *All threads used in these projects are by Sulky of America.*

BONUS PROJECTS on CD:
Striped and Spotted Napkins
Sandals Tote Bag
Striped Straw Tote Bag

Fall Harvest

The bountiful harvest season is a great time of year to celebrate with a dinner or cocktail party. Use a twin-size bed quilt as a warm backdrop for your linens, and cover it with the table runner embroidered with harvest themes. For a cocktail party, give your guests embroidered stemware marker charms for their glasses. For a dinner party, embroider on purchased napkins and place mats for easy, elegant sophistication.

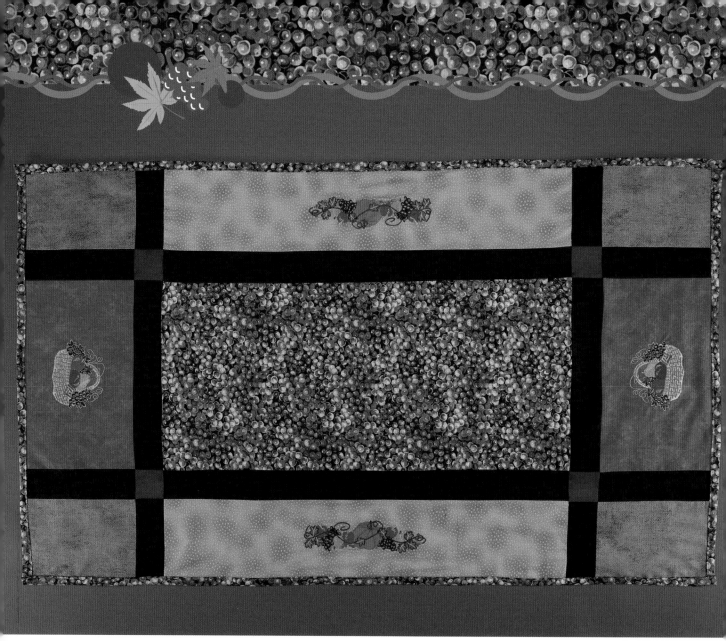

Autumn Table Runner

This fall table runner in rich colors brings the harvest right to your table. The center of the runner is a colorful cotton print, and the embroidered patches around the edge are stitched on fabrics that complement the center panel.

Supplies:

2 yd. print fabric

⅓ yd. fabric for side panels

¼ yd. fabric for end panels

Pumpkin with Grapes and Fruit Basket embroidery designs

Tear-away stabilizer

40-wt. embroidery thread

4 pieces of fabric for corners, each 4½" x 6½"

¼ yd. fabric for sashing

4 pieces contrasting fabric for sashing, each 2" square

1¼ yd. flannel

Bias tape maker (optional)

Directions:

Note: all seam allowances are ¼".

1 Cut two pieces of fabric large enough to fit in the hoop and at least 22¼" wide for the side panels. Hoop one piece of the fabric with the stabilizer, place the embroidery design in the center, and stitch the Pumpkin and Grapes design. Remove from the hoop and tear away the stabilizer. Cut the fabric 4½" high x 22¼" wide, keeping the embroidery in the center. Repeat with the second side panel.

2 Cut two pieces of fabric large enough to fit in the hoop and at least 10¼" wide for the end panels. Hoop one piece of the fabric with the stabilizer, place the embroidery design in the center, and stitch the Fruit Basket design. Remove from the hoop and tear away the stabilizer. Cut the fabric 6½" high x 10¼" wide, keeping the embroidery in the center. Repeat with the second end panel.

3 Cut the print fabric 10¼" x 22¼" for the center of the table runner. Cut the sashing fabric into two pieces 2" x 22¼", two pieces 2" x 10¼", four pieces 2" x 4½" and four pieces 2" x 6½".

4 With right sides together, sew one 22¼" sashing piece to one long side of the center section. Sew the other 22¼" piece to the opposite side of the center section. Sew the sashing strip on one side to the embroidered side panel. Repeat with the remaining side panel. Press all seam allowances open.

5 With right sides together, sew one end of a 10¼" sashing strip to a contrasting fabric 2" square, followed by a 4½" sashing strip. Sew another 2" square to the other end of the longer sashing strip, again followed by a 4½" strip. Repeat with the other pieces for the other end of the runner. Press seam allowances open.

6 Sew each pieced strip to the ends of the center section/side panels with right sides together, matching the 2" squares to the sashing strips of the center section. Press seam allowances open.

7 With right sides together, sew two 6½" sashing strips to each side of one of the end panels. Sew a corner piece to the other side of a 6½" strip. Sew another corner piece to the sashing strip at the other side. Repeat with the remaining sashing strips, end panels and corner pieces. Press all seam allowances open.

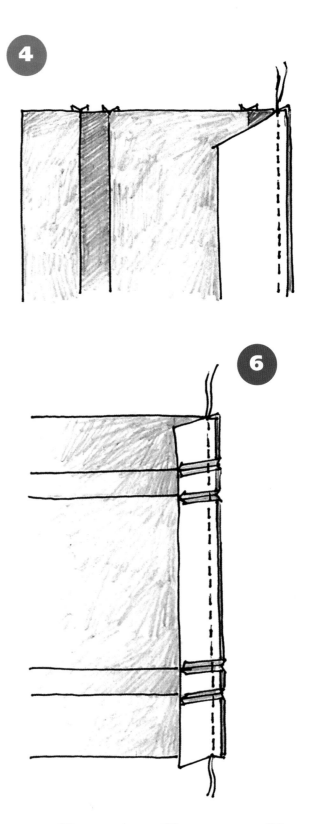

8 With right sides together, sew each end panel/corner piece section to each end of the center section/side panels, matching the sashing strips of the end panels to the 2" squares. Press seam allowances open.

9 Cut a piece of flannel and print fabric the same size as the top of the table runner. Place the wrong side of the top over the flannel. Place the wrong side of the backing fabric on the other side of the flannel, and baste around the edges.

10 With the remaining print fabric, cut two 2" x 22" and two 2" x 38" bias strips for the binding, piecing if necessary. Place each strip in a bias tape maker and press. Fold in half lengthwise to create a ½" folded strip. Place the ends of the runner in the shorter bias strips and stitch. Place the sides of the runner in the longer bias strips and stitch, folding in the short ends before stitching.

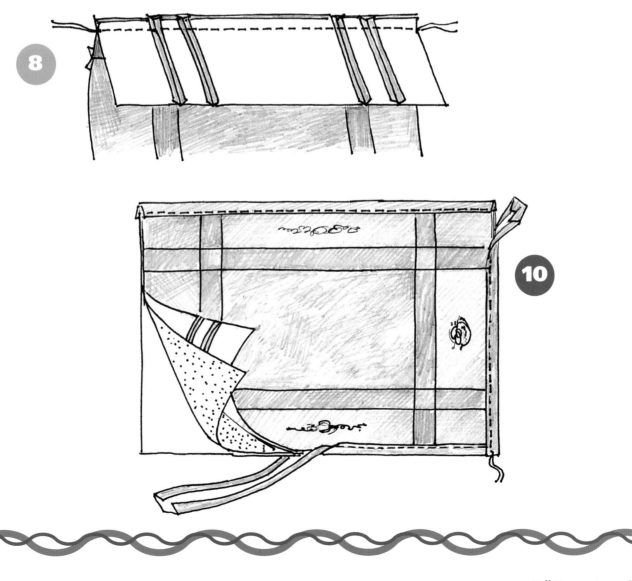

Stemware Marker Charms

These colorful charms will decorate and help identify your guests' glasses.
Use memory wire rings, and place beads on each side of the embroidery.
The end of the wire is capped with metal, but you can bend back the end
of the wire to hold the beads instead.

Supplies for four charms:

Cut-away stabilizer

Stemware Marker embroidery design

40-wt. embroidery thread

4 silver memory wire rings

4 silver memory wire ends

Fast-drying glue

Seed beads in a variety of colors,
    approximately 1 tsp. for two markers

Wire cutter

Awl or other sharp, pointed tool

Directions:

1 Place one or two pieces of stabilizer in the hoop. Stitch the Stemware Marker design and remove from the hoop. Cut carefully around each of the markers, discarding the small scroll design in the center. (It is included if you wish to use the design as a whole.)

2 Cut the wire ring so that you only have one loop with the ends slightly overlapping. Glue a wire end to one end of the ring. Let dry.

3 Put beads on the wire ring until you have reached halfway around the ring. Poke a hole with the awl in the center of the embroidered circle at the top of the marker, and put the ring through it, stopping at the beads. Continue threading the beads on the wire until ¼" of the wire remains. Glue another wire end to the end of the ring, and let dry.

Pumpkin Place Mat and Napkin

Spice up purchased matching place mats and napkins with machine embroidery!

Buy inexpensive linens at store sales to use as gifts or for last-minute get-togethers.

Supplies for one place mat and napkin:

Purchased place mat

Purchased napkin

Adhesive stabilizer

Pumpkin Topiary design

40-wt. embroidery thread

Directions:

1 Place the stabilizer in the hoop and peel off the paper to expose the sticky surface. Baste the design on the stabilizer without any thread or fabric to find the outline of the design in the hoop.

2 Determine placement of the design on your place mat by marking the outer and lower edges with a pin. Line up the markings on the place mat over the sticky surface in the hoop. Baste with thread in the machine to hold your place mat in place.

3 Stitch the design; remove from the hoop and press.

4 For the napkin, hoop the stabilizer and remove the paper to expose the sticky surface.

5 Decide on the placement of the pumpkin on the corner of your napkin. You will only stitch the large pumpkin of the Pumpkin Topiary design. Place the napkin corner over the sticky surface in the hoop and stitch steps 4, 5 and 6 of the design.

6 Remove from the hoop and press.

Golden Bread Cover

Keep fresh-from-the-oven rolls warm with this quick and easy bread cover.

This project has embroidery in one corner and is lined with a different fabric print for added color.

Supplies:

18" square of fabric

18" square of fabric for back

Fruit Basket embroidery design

Tear-away stabilizer

40-wt. embroidery thread

Directions:

1 Hoop the fabric and the stabilizer so that the center of the design will be placed 5" from one corner. Embroider the design and remove from the hoop. Tear away the stabilizer and press.

2 With right sides together and a ¼" seam allowance, sew the cover to the backing fabric around all edges, leaving a small opening for turning. Clip the corners; turn to the right side and press. Stitch the opening closed.

Other Ideas:

1 For coasters, stitch the Stemware Marker designs separately on felt, using the Coaster pattern in the Game Night chapter.

2 Stitch the Wine Glass Cheers design onto fabric for a classy invitation.

3 Stitch only the inside motifs of the Stemware Markers designs for place cards.

4 The Pumpkin Topiary can be stitched to the pocket of an apron or on a flatware holder for holiday dinners.

> • *All threads used in these projects are by Sulky of America.*

BONUS PROJECTS on CD:
Cocktail Napkin
Harvest Basket Liner

Fairy Gathering

Girls of all ages will want to attend this party! Plan a fairy gathering as a birthday party for little girls or as an afternoon tea party for the young at heart. The centerpiece is easier to make than it looks, but if you prefer, use a floral bouquet to hold the embroidered fairies and butterflies instead. Give fairy wands to each guest, and let the magic begin!

Maypole Centerpiece

I found this maypole design in an old 1890s women's magazine
and adapted it using today's materials. The pole fits into a container of Plaster of Paris
and has a metal ring suspended from the top with wires and a screw. Cover it with floral tape
and artificial flowers, and hide the butterflies and fairies among the blossoms.

Supplies:

4"-high x 6"-diameter basket

Plastic container to fit inside basket

Plaster of Paris

20" dowel, ⅝" diameter

Screw, 1½" to 2" long

8"-diameter metal ring

Floral tape

1 yd. 30-gauge covered wire

4 yd. ribbon, 1" wide

6 ft. narrow star garland

Fast-drying glue

Iridescent shred (sold with gift wrap)

Artificial flowers

Heavy cut-away stabilizer

40-wt. embroidery thread

Fairy and Butterflies embroidery designs

Lightweight wire for embroidered designs

Glue

Directions:

1 Wrap the dowel with floral tape, stopping about 5" from one end. Fill the container with Plaster of Paris and insert the unwrapped end of the dowel into the center. Let dry.

2 Wrap the metal ring with floral tape. Cut wire into four equal pieces. Wrap one end of the wire around the ring. Repeat with another piece of wire directly across from the first wrapping. Repeat with the remaining wires at 90-degree angles from the first two wires.

3 Screw the screw into the top of the dowel so that the head is about ¼" from the dowel. Wrap the loose wires around the screw — each wire length should be 6" between the dowel and the ring.

4 Cut the ribbon into four equal pieces. Glue each piece to the top of the screw and over one of the wires.

5 Cut the blossoms off the floral stems. Glue the blossoms around the ring and the dowel. Wrap lengths of the star garland around the pole and the ring.

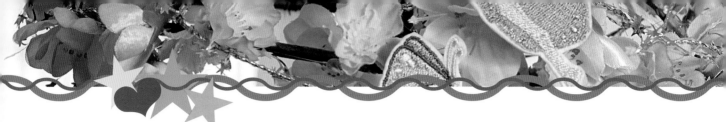

6 Hoop the stabilizer, and embroider at least three sets of Butterflies and two Fairies.

7 Remove from the hoop and cut around each shape approximately ¹⁄₁₆" from the stitching.

8 Cut a 2" to 3" piece of wire for each motif, and glue one end to the back of the motif. Place the motifs where desired and wrap the wire around a floral stem. Glue to the floral stem if necessary.

Sparkling Napkins and Napkin Rings

The napkins are made from lovely pink and purple fabric.
The napkin rings are lengths of the star garland twisted in a circle several times.
Glue embroidered butterflies to the ends of the garland,
and they will appear to be flying off the table!

Supplies for one napkin and one napkin ring:

15" square of print fabric

15" of narrow star garland

Butterflies embroidery design

Heavy cut-away stabilizer

40-wt. embroidery thread

Fabric glue

Napkin:

1 Serge, zigzag stitch or pink around all of the edges.

2 Press the edges ½" to the wrong side. Topstitch around the edges ⅜" from the fold.

Napkin Ring:

1 Hoop the stabilizer and stitch one set of butterflies.

2 Remove from the hoop and cut around the motifs, approximately ¹⁄₁₆" from the stitching.

3 Beginning 3"- 4" from one end, wrap the wire into a circle twice around your fingers so that you have 3"- 4" remaining at the other end. Twist the ends together and bend the wire slightly. Glue one butterfly to each end of the garland.

Fairy Dust Bag

Fill these bags with candy or other treats for your guests to enjoy.

Use a shiny fabric, like satin, for a dazzling effect.

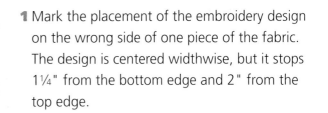

Supplies for one bag:

2 pieces of satin fabric, 5½" high x 4" wide

Fairy Wand embroidery design

Adhesive stabilizer

40-wt. embroidery thread

½ yd. cording, ¼" wide

8" metallic lace trim, ¾" wide

8" piece of double-fold bias tape

Directions:

1 Mark the placement of the embroidery design on the wrong side of one piece of the fabric. The design is centered widthwise, but it stops 1¼" from the bottom edge and 2" from the top edge.

2 Hoop the stabilizer and tear away the paper. Baste the outline of the design without thread on the stabilizer to mark the position of the design. Place the fabric over the stabilizer and embroider the Fairy Wand design. Tear away the stabilizer and remove from the hoop.

3 With right sides together and a ¼" seam allowance, sew the front of the bag to the remaining piece of satin along one side edge. Press seam allowances open.

4 Press the top edge of the bag ¼" to the wrong side. Place the straight edge of the lace just under the pressed edge and stitch.

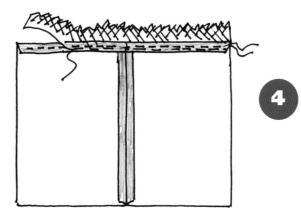

5 Using a ¼" seam allowance, stitch the remaining side seam at the top for ½". Leave the side seam open for another ½". Continue stitching the side seam and bottom edge. Press seam allowances open.

6 Make a casing for the cord by stitching both sides of the bias tape ½" from the top edge of the fabric, turning the ends under at the open area of the seam allowance.

7 Thread the cording from the outside of the bag, through the casing, and back out through the opening. Tie a knot in the ends.

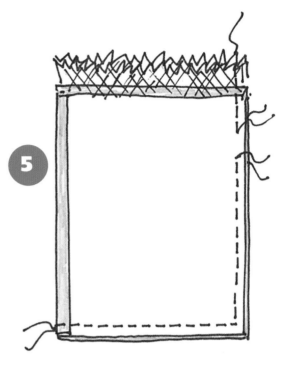

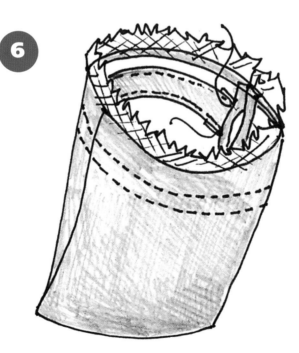

Pink Picture Frame

You can find inexpensive, unfinished picture frames at craft stores.
Take pictures of each of your guests as a remembrance of the magical event,
and place the photos in these painted and embroidered keepsakes.

Supplies:

Unfinished wooden picture frame

Fairy House and Butterflies embroidery designs

Heavy cut-away stabilizer

40-wt. embroidery thread

Paint for frame

Glitter paint for topcoat

Glue

Directions:

1 Paint the frame the desired color with two coats. When dry, paint again with glitter paint. Let dry.

2 Hoop the stabilizer and embroider the Butterflies and the Fairy House. Remove from hoop, and cut around the motifs approximately $1/16$" away from the stitching.

3 Glue the Fairy House to the lower right side, and glue the Butterflies to the upper left side of the frame.

Other Ideas:

1 Stitch any of the designs to children's clothing, such as a nightgown or jumper.

2 All of the designs can be used to decorate a girl's bedroom. Embroider bed linens or create cut-outs and glue them to a mirror.

3 Use the Fairy and Wand designs on a tooth fairy pillow.

- *All threads used in these projects are by Madeira USA.*

- *The fairy print and coordinating floral print fabrics are by Timeless Treasures Fabrics, Inc.*

**BONUS PROJECT on CD:
Purple Place Mat**

Mardi Gras!

Bring drama into your dining room with an opulent Mardi Gras gala event! Use a dramatic cotton print for the table covering, and top it with a glittering gold cloth. Add a table runner with harlequin-style patches, place mats, and a fabulously flamboyant centerpiece. Lavish use of beads, coins and feathers will make this a night to remember!

Mask Centerpiece

*The Large Mask embroidery design turns a simple glass container
into an attention-grabbing centerpiece. Fill the vase with colored glass stones
and an assortment of feathers, foil sprays, beads and more. Add crystals to the gold dots
in the design for even more sparkle, and let the party begin!*

Supplies:

Scrap black cotton fabric large enough to fit in embroidery hoop

Black cut-away stabilizer

Large Mask embroidery design

40-wt. embroidery thread

Seam sealant, such as Fray Block

3 mm rhinestones, if desired

Fabric glue

Flat-sided vase

Colored glass stones or marbles

Feathers, foil sprays, beads, etc. to fill vase

Directions:

1 Hoop the fabric with one or two pieces of stabilizer, depending on the results of your test of the design. Embroider the design and remove from the hoop.

2 Cut around the design, leaving approximately ½" of fabric around the outside. Apply seam sealant on the fabric just outside of the design and let dry.

3 Carefully cut around the design, leaving the eye holes.

4 Glue or heat-set the rhinestones randomly over a few of the dots on the mask.

5 Glue the mask to the outside of the vase.

6 Fill the vase with colored stones. Place an assortment of feathers, beads, etc. inside the vase.

Tasseled Table Runner

This richly-decorated table runner has a harlequin print in the center
with three embroidery designs on the diamond-shaped patches at either end.
To make the runner shorter, shorten the length of the center panel.
Add tassels at the ends for an elegant look.

Supplies:

2 yd. cotton print fabric

¼ yd. each blue, green and purple cotton fabric

½ yd. black cotton fabric

Small Mask, Fleur de Lis and Jester Hat embroidery designs

Black cut-away stabilizer

40-wt. embroidery thread

Seam sealant, such as Fray Block

2 yd. medium-weight fusible interfacing

2 tassels, 3" long

Directions:

Note: all seam allowances are ¼".

1 From the printed fabric, cut the center of the table runner 15" x 36". Cut two border strips 2" x 36", and two more border strips 2" x 18" of black fabric.

2 Sew the long strips to the sides of the table runner, with right sides together. Press seam allowances open. Sew the short strips to each end of the table runner using a ¼" seam allowance. Press seam allowances open.

3 Cut six pieces of black fabric large enough to fit inside the hoop. Hoop the fabric and one or two pieces of the stabilizer. Embroider two Jester Hats, two Small Masks, and two Fleur de Lis designs on each piece. Trim each of them to be a 4½" square turned on point to be a diamond shape.

4 Cut two blue 4½" squares, two green 4½" squares and three purple 4½" squares. These will become diamond-shaped patches.

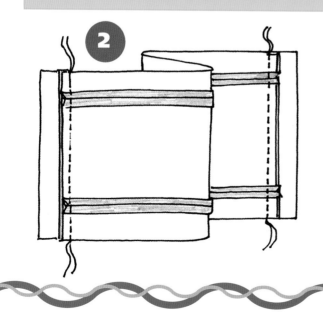

5 With right sides together, sew the upper right side of one of the Fleur de Lis embroidered diamonds to a green diamond, then the lower left side of a Small Mask diamond, followed by a purple diamond. Press seam allowances open.

6 Sew a blue diamond to a purple diamond, followed by another blue diamond. Press seam allowances open.

7 Sew the upper right side of the Jester Hat diamond to a green diamond. Press seam allowances open.

8 Sew the first strip to the second one, beginning with the blue diamond next to the upper left side of the Fleur de Lis diamond. Sew this to the third strip, beginning with the lower right side of the Jester Hat next to the blue diamond. Sew the purple diamond to the upper left side of the Jester Hat patch.

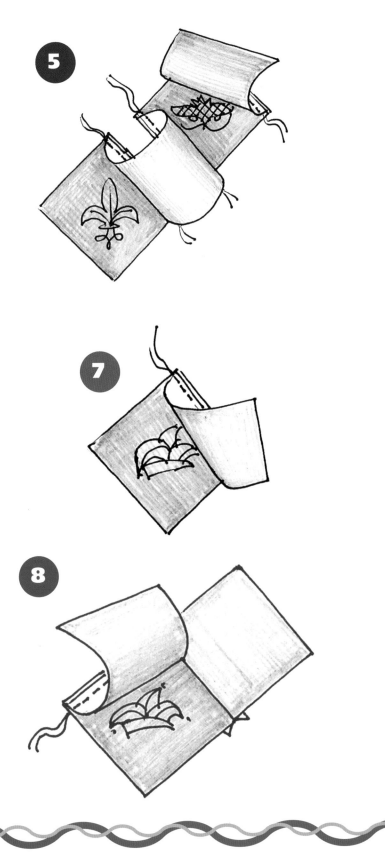

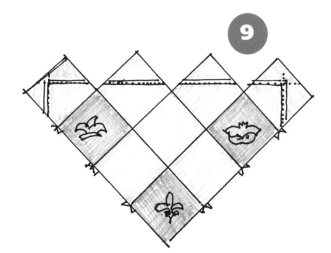

9 Trim the solid color squares at the top of the patchwork, ¼" beyond the points of the black embroidered diamonds. Mark the center of the purple diamonds at the sides, and draw a horizontal line ¼" beyond the center and trim.

10 With right sides together, sew the patchwork to the 18" black strip at one end. Press seam allowances open.

11 Repeat steps 3-10 for the other side of the runner.

12 Trace the outline of the runner to the wrong side of the remaining print fabric for the back. Cut a piece of interfacing ¼" smaller than the back runner on all sides. Fuse the interfacing to the back runner, following manufacturer's instructions.

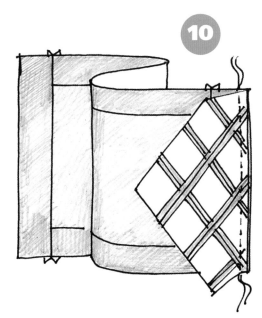

13 Sew the front to the back, placing the tassels at the points at the ends. Leave an opening for turning. Clip the points; trim the seam allowances, and turn to the right side. Press.

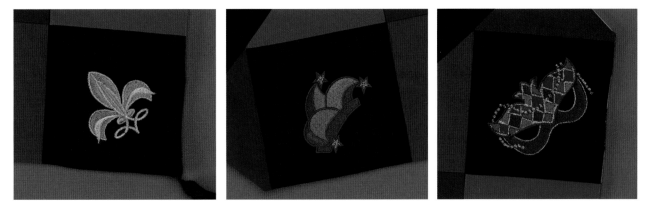

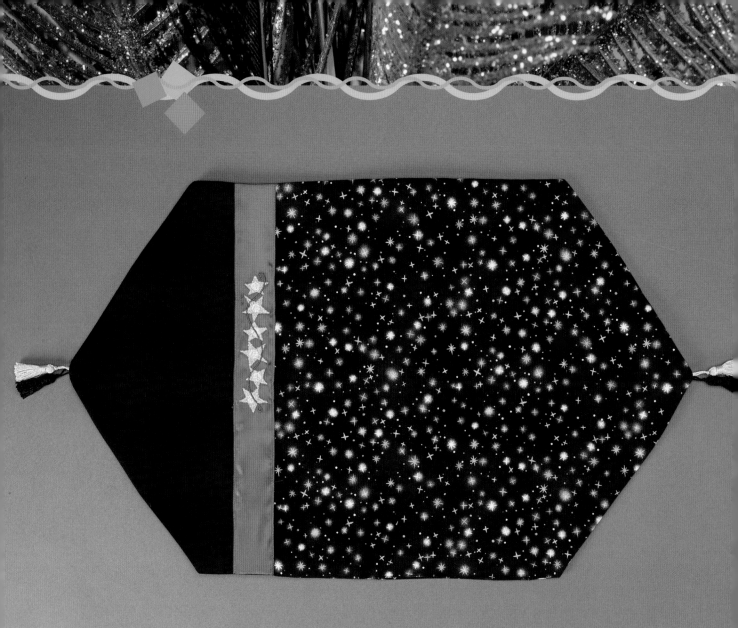

Starry Place Mat

Combine fabrics to give ordinary place mats a brand-new look!

The seam is covered by an embroidered satin ribbon.

Make the sides of the place mat come to a point

and add decorative tassels.

Supplies for one place mat:

½ yd. printed cotton fabric

7½" x 14" piece of solid color fabric

½ yd. ribbon, 1½" wide

Stars embroidery design

Adhesive stabilizer

40-wt. embroidery thread

½ yd. fusible interfacing

4 tassels, 1½" long

Directions:

1 Place the stabilizer in the hoop and tear off the paper on top. Place the ribbon over the stabilizer so that the design will be stitched approximately 4" from one end of the ribbon. Stitch the design and remove from the stabilizer. Press.

2 Cut a 16" wide x 14" high piece of the printed fabric. Find the 7" mark on the right side edge of the fabric. From the right edge, find the 5" mark on both the top and bottom edges. Draw a line from the 7" mark to both 5" marks on the top and bottom edges. Cut along these lines to create a point. Repeat this step to make a point on the left side of the solid color fabric.

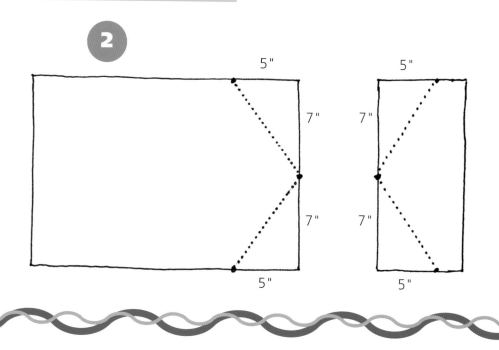

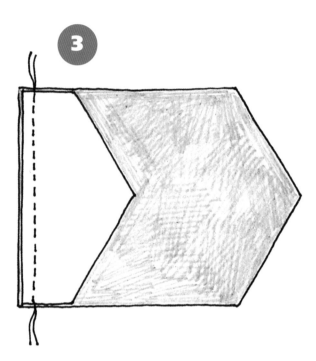

3 With right sides together and a ½" seam allowance, sew both pieces of the place mat front
together along the straight side edges. Press
seam allowances open. Place the ribbon over
the seam so that the embroidery is 3½" from
the top edge. Stitch along both sides of the
ribbon.

4 Place the place mat over the remaining print
fabric and cut around the edges to make the
back. Cut the interfacing ½" smaller on all
sides than the place mat back. Fuse the interfacing to the back, following manufacturer's
instructions.

5 Place the front and back place mats right sides
together, and pin two tassels at each point on
the sides. Stitch with a ½" seam allowance,
leaving an opening at the bottom of the place
mat. Clip the points; turn to the right side and
press. Stitch the opening closed.

Embellished Mask

*All of your guests can have masks to wear at the party or keep as a party remembrance.
These inexpensive masks, available at party stores, are decorated with the Jester Hat
embroidery design and feathers at one corner. Rhinestone stars are glued over the
stars in the embroidery motif for more pizzazz.*

Supplies for one mask:

Plain black mask

Jester Hat embroidery design

Scrap black cotton fabric large enough to fit in embroidery hoop

Black cut-away stabilizer

40-wt. embroidery thread

Seam sealant, such as Fray Block

Small feathers

Six 14 mm stars

Fabric glue

Directions:

1 Hoop the fabric with one or two pieces of stabilizer, depending on the results of your test of the design. Embroider the design and remove from the hoop.

2 Cut around the design, leaving approximately ½" of fabric around the outside. Apply seam sealant on the fabric just outside of the design. Let dry.

3 Carefully cut around the design. Glue three stars to the stars in the hat.

4 Glue three or four feathers at one of the corners of the mask. Glue the embroidered hat over the feathers. Glue three stars to the opposite corner where desired.

Other Ideas:

1 The Fleur de Lis is a classic motif that can be applied to pillows and other home décor items.

2 Stitch the Small Mask design in other colors for Halloween or New Year's celebrations.

3 The Stars embroidery is great for linens or a candle wrap for New Year's Eve parties. You could also place it on one or two sides of a picture frame.

- *Sulky threads were used for all the projects, with the addition of Superior Threads gold metallic thread.*

- *All fabrics, except for the sheer gold fabric, are by Robert Kaufman Fabrics.*

BONUS PROJECTS on CD:
Fleur-de-lis Napkin and Napkin Ring

Milestones

All of us celebrate milestone occasions throughout our lives, and this chapter will give you ideas for those special celebrations. Mix and match the embroidery designs to suit your needs, or use your imagination to create your own unique decorations.

Unity Candle Wrap

Stitch the beautiful Scroll embroidery design to a candle wrap for a loved one's wedding.
To personalize the decoration, use colors that match the bridal party. You could also use several
candles with this embroidered wrap in your home to decorate a mantel.

Supplies:

3"-wide candle, 9" tall

¼ yd. fabric

Scroll embroidery design

Tear-away stabilizer

40-wt. embroidery thread

3½" x 10¼" piece of medium-weight fusible interfacing

⅔ yd. metallic lace, ⅝" wide

2½" Velcro strip

Directions:

1 Cut the fabric large enough to fit inside the hoop and at least 11" wide. Hoop the fabric with the stabilizer and stitch the design. Remove from the hoop and press.

2 Cut the embroidered fabric 4" x 10¾" wide, with the embroidery in the center. Cut another piece of fabric the same dimensions for the back.

3 Center the interfacing on the wrong side of the back, and fuse according to the manufacturer's instructions. Stitch the back to the front along one long edge with right sides together and a ¼" seam allowance. Open out, and press the ends of both the front and back ¼" to the wrong side. Press the remaining long edge of the front and back ¼" to the wrong side. Fold them together and stitch close to the pressed edge of the long edge and both side edges.

4 Cut lace to fit the long edges of the candle wrap, including an extra ¼" at both ends. Stitch the lace to the long edges, turning the ends under ¼".

5 Try the candle wrap on your candle, overlapping right to left to determine Velcro placement. Stitch Velcro to each end.

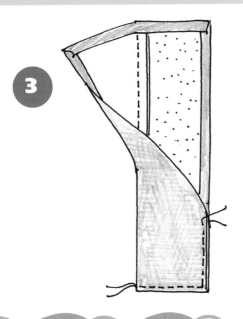

Guest Book Cover

*This cover is the right size to fit a standard guest book used
for weddings, retirement parties or other formal events.
Personalize your book cover by adding names and dates
above or below the embroidery design.*

Supplies:

Guest book, approximately 6" x 8"

½ yd. fabric

Hearts embroidery design

Tear-away stabilizer

40-wt. embroidery thread

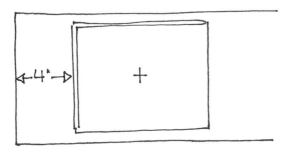

Directions:

1 Measure the guest book to be covered. Cut a piece of fabric ½" wider than the book and 4" longer at each end. This should be approximately 7" high x 24" wide. Trace the outline of the front of the book on the wrong side of the fabric so that 4" extends beyond the front. Find the center inside the markings. This will be the center of your design.

2 Hoop the fabric with the stabilizer and stitch the design. Remove from the hoop and tear away the stabilizer. Press.

3 Cut another piece of fabric the same size as the front for the lining. With right sides together and a ¼" seam allowance, stitch around all edges, leaving a small opening for turning. Clip the corners; turn to the right side and press. Stitch the opening closed.

4 Place the book inside the cover and fold the ends to the inside of each cover. Pin in place. Stitch along the entire top and bottom edges close to the edge, including the folded ends that have become pockets. Slide the guest book inside the pockets.

Ring Bearer Pillow

This simple and elegant pillow holds rings inside the embroidered wreath.

Add tassels or beads at the corners for more elaborate embellishment.

Supplies:

½ yd. fabric

Wreath embroidery design

Tear-away stabilizer

40-wt. embroidery thread

12" pillow form

1½ yd. ribbon, ⅛" wide

Directions:

1 Cut two 12½" square pieces of fabric for the front and back. Hoop one piece of fabric with the stabilizer and stitch the design in the center of the fabric. Remove from the hoop and tear away the stabilizer. Press.

2 With right sides together and a ¼" seam allowance, sew around all edges of the front and back pillow covers, leaving an opening for turning. Clip the corners; turn to the right side and press.

3 Insert the pillow form. Pin the opening closed, and slipstitch by hand or sew by machine.

4 Cut the ribbon in half and find the center of each half. Stitch both pieces to the center of the wreath design, and tie the rings on with a bow.

Heirloom Napkin

*You can find napkins from days gone by at antique shops.
Embroider the classic Greek Key embroidery design in one corner,
matching the colors of your china, and these personalized napkins
will be ready for any special event.*

Supplies:

Vintage napkin, any size

Adhesive stabilizer

Greek Key embroidery design

40-wt. embroidery thread

Directions:

1 Place the sticky stabilizer in the hoop and tear away the paper. Baste the outline of the design without thread on the stabilizer to mark the position of the design.

2 Mark the design area on your napkin. (I stitched mine 2" from the hemstitching on the edge.) Place the corner of the napkin on the marked area of the stabilizer. Baste the outline of the design with thread to keep the napkin in place if you are sure the napkin fabric is stable and the needle holes can be pressed out.

3 Stitch the design and remove from the stabilizer. Press.

Other Ideas:

1 Make the Wreath design in red and green for the holidays, and use it on a pillow, table runner or wall hanging. It can also be made with a monogram inside for a pillow or wedding photo album cover.

2 Stitch the Celebrate design on a greeting card.

3 Embroider the Scroll design on a frame, the back of a jacket, the end of a table runner or on an album cover.

4 Stitch the Hearts design for Valentine's Day on a greeting card or border on a place mat.

5 Isolate the center heart in the Hearts design for an ornament, greeting card or corner of a napkin.

6 Use the Greek Key design as a border of a frame, placing the design in all four corners.

• *Rayon threads used in these projects are by Sulky of America and the metallic threads are by Superior Threads.*

BONUS PROJECT on CD: Celebration Frame

CD-ROM Contents
Embroidery Design Index

Birthday Bash

Balloons
5 colors, 8 color changes

Cake
9 colors,
14 color changes

Happy Birthday
4 colors

Party Hat with Star
5 colors, 6 color changes

Party Hat with Stripes
5 colors, 8 color changes

Present
5 colors, 6 color changes

Tea in the Garden

Garland
8 colors, 9 color changes

Large Bouquet
10 colors,
13 color changes

Small Bouquet
9 colors,
12 color changes

Straw Hat
6 colors

Teapot
5 colors

Game Night

Four Suits
3 colors,
16 color changes

**Four Suits
(Club, Diamond,
Heart and Spade)**
3 colors, 4 color changes

Joker Hat
2 colors, 4 color changes

Day at the Beach

Fish
6 colors, 7 color changes

Flip Flop
7 colors, 9 color changes

Hibiscus
7 colors

Orange Slice
4 colors

Small Zinnia
4 colors

Umbrella
6 colors,
10 color changes

Watermelon
4 colors

Zinnia
4 colors

Fall Harvest

Cheers Wine Glass
3 colors, 4 color changes

Fruit Basket
10 colors,
13 color changes

Pumpkin Topiary
7 colors,
14 color changes

Pumpkin with Grapes
9 colors,
10 color changes

Stemware Marker
12 colors,
27 color changes

Fairy Gathering

Butterfly
4 colors, 5 color changes

Fairy
6 colors, 9 color changes

Fairy House
5 colors, 6 color changes

Fairy Wand
2 colors

Mardi Gras!

Stars
3 colors

Jester Hat
4 colors

Small Mask
4 colors, 7 color changes

Fleur de Lis
2 colors

Large Mask
3 colors

Milestones

Wreath
3 colors

Hearts
3 colors, 4 color changes

Scroll
2 colors, 3 color changes

Celebrate
2 colors

Greek Key
3 colors

Resources

Contributors

The following companies supplied products for use in this book:

Aurifil Threads
Tristan Embroidery Supplies Inc.
800-847-3230
www.tristan.bc.ca
Threads for Birthday Bash

Camelot Cottons
Division of Eugene Textiles
www.eugenetextiles.ca
Printed fabrics for Birthday Bash

CheepTrims.com
877-BUY-TRIM
www.cheeptrims.com
Pompom fringe for Birthday Bash

Madeira
www.madeirausa.com
Tea in the Garden, Fairy Gathering threads

Mary's Productions
800-562-5578
www.marymulari.com
Apron pattern for Tea in the Garden

RNK Distributing (Floriani Products)
877-331-0034
www.rnkdistributing.com
Stabilizers

Robert Kaufman Fabrics
800-877-2066
www.robertkaufman.com
All fabrics in Mardi Gras!
(except metallic gold fabric)

Robison-Anton Textile Company
www.robison-anton.com
Game Night threads

Sulky of America
800-874-4115
www.sulky.com
Stabilizers, KK 2000, and Fall Harvest,
Milestones and Day at the Beach threads

Superior Threads
800-499-1777
www.superiorthreads.com
Metallic threads

Timeless Treasures
www.ttfabrics.com
Fairy print fabrics in Fairy Gathering

Walnut Hollow Farm, Inc.
800-950-5101
www.walnuthollow.com
Textile Tool

Warm Company
800-234-WARM
www.warmcompany.com
Insul-Bright

About the Author

As the owner of Fancywork and Fashion, Joan has written thirteen books about sewing and embroidery, including *Sew Today's Fashions for 18-Inch Dolls* and *Sew Baby Doll Clothes*. She publishes a quarterly newsletter that includes patterns, tips and more for people who love sewing for dolls. Cactus Punch and VSM Sewing, Inc. have released embroidery discs with Joan's embroidery designs for dolls, and this book gave Joan an exciting new opportunity to create machine embroidery for another passion, entertaining and seasonal décor.

Joan loves to travel the country sharing her knowledge of sewing and embroidery. Her work has been shown in *Designs in Machine Embroidery, Sew Beautiful,* and *Creative Needle* magazines, and she has made an appearance on the PBS series, "America Sews with Sue Hausmann." Joan and her husband reside in Minnesota. With two grown children, they are thoroughly enjoying their empty nest.

Make the Most
of Your Embroidery Machine

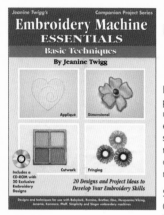